angel voices

The poetry of Scott Hastie

Angel Voices by Scott Hastie
First published 2014
Centuria, London UK

ISBN: 9780950977072
E book ISBN: 9780950977089

A catalogue record for this book is available from the British Library

Printed in the UK

Designed by *raygun*

facebook.com/scotthastiespiritpoet
twitter @scotthastiepoet

www.scotthastie.com

Sublime moments refracted,
Even if only for seconds,
Caught forever in your soul...

Age gathers, colludes.
Cadences fade fitfully,
Seemingly before their time.

But there are echoes still,
Shapes we inherit,
We inhabit, we bequeath.

A life however bravely spent,
Will always be jagged, incomplete,
Never far away
From being enveloped in darkness.

Some may say,
Especially those who've known joy in life,
That this is not right.

I tell you clearly they are wrong.

So, just as a dancer
Might spin for you an exact pirouette
And release themselves in the perfect burst,
A lingering silhouette of energy,
Be content to love, to dazzle in the light,
If only for moments...

And then be gone,
With gladness in your heart,
Before the creeping shadows
Claim too much your sadness at leaving.

Marks are made.

Despite ourselves
We etch away,
We leave behind.

A few might even dare
To place something
Proudly on the landscape,
Just for its own sake,
Or so that afterwards
They might be spoken of
By strangers.

But, either way,
It matters not.
For when our souls
Are open
Connections occur.

Perhaps there is a clue here,
A hint
Of something more fluid,
More oceanic.
A fugue state
That makes more sense
Of all this,
Our pattern, our purpose,
Our struggle to be serene...

For David

Needing love,
We squeeze what we can
From a fluid landscape of life and light,
Gifted to us but for a moment
In the grand scheme of things.

Hope glistens,
Daring us to do so much more.

And, at our best,
When least distracted
By the petty cares of the day,
We hunger for a constant,
To find a flow,
A warm, healing current
We can swim within.

One soul's odyssey
In search of a tipping point.

The possibility of honour,
The chance of grace in our lives.

A busy city,
Far from home.

Onrushing,
The teeming crowd,
A tsunami of sorts.

And as you walk on into the melee,
As it comes to you,
For the briefest, sweetest of moments
To catch the eye,
To share a smile,
To touch the soul of a stranger
You may never see again.

This is as it should be.

The often cavernously empty
Business of life will always
Occasionally be overwhelmed by truth.
For the restless soul
Hungers for such moorings,
Such absolute points of recognition
Gifted by love,
By light shared with others.

But such chances come and go so suddenly
That what was once so recent, so vivid
Already seems so distant and long ago.

What then,
If not still true to your heart?

Only swamped I fear.
Lost on a surging tide,
Swept back to faceless oblivion,
To the ruin of indifference to start again...

What are we if not set apart,
Divided?
Born, fractured by birth,
Into this place
Of limit and misapprehension,
Seemingly doomed before we begin.

But our salvation
Is the element of precognition,
Glowing seeds of foreknowledge,
Eons old, we all still carry within us,
That just sit awaiting triggers,
Resonance.
Dormant in our soul
Every single moment we live and breathe.

Whilst, all the while,
And at a very necessary distance
From any individual orbit,
Seemingly indifferent
To the apparent cruelties of life,
Beyond all oxygen of hope
And the dark suffocation of loss and despair,
There are the most exquisite patterns
At work here,
Huge beyond our imagining.

Patterns, however intricate, that fit.
And between them gaps, potentials,
Knowing rhythms, inevitabilities
That lock together and spin,
Lock and spin endlessly
To make this our tempting,
Transitory life
And all our chances possible.

The truth is, in the face of such fractal grandeur,
The needs of any one of us are not many.

Ultimately the challenge is simply
One of love and generosity
That brings all things together again.

Just to be open and joyful in your heart,
To have grace and compassion,
To trust that what people call God
Can be found in the spaces in between.

However beautiful,
No pebble on the beach.

You were my touchstone.

And yes,
I have now smelt the perfume of the Gods.

If only for precious moments
Opened the gilded door
And walked through.

Set foot on hallowed ground,
Taken refuge where my soul longed to be,
In the sunlit meadow of my dreams.

Bathed in love and light,
Healed and nourished,
Elevated by experiences of wonder.

It was the miracle of how the needs,
The spiritual hunger
Of two separate physical beings,
Two fractured souls,
Could fit together so perfectly,
Like long lost pieces of some ancient code
That, once re-united, yielded up energies,
Ecstasies and insights beyond our imagining.

That was the key.

And far beyond any love affair
With its own predictable half-life
Of intensity, its cycle of emotion.

Instead a permanent path
That, once illuminated,
Goes ever onward – a way home...

And still the darkness waits for me,
As I know it will...
And ever more avariciously still,
As it senses my journey comes closer to fruition.

I know in my heart it is a given
That I can never entirely banish
This spectre of the night,
It will always be beside me, as it needs to be.

Just as surely as the sunniest of summer's mornings
Or the broadest of smiles on a lover's face
Can make your heart soar,
As a counterpoint in the navigation
Of all that's possible in life.
All that one would ever want to reach out for,
Whether driven by angels or demons.

So I choose to condemn it
To wait on the sidelines forever.
And as an irrelevance, a meaningless shadow,
A token silhouette to all my blessings.

Like the soft dusting of fallen snow on hollow bones,
On the already broken, spilt corpse
Of souls long since departed.
Strengthened by the certainty
That the light I cherish and hold dear within
Will instead keep me safe and warm,
Till my own time comes...

Sometimes illuminations come to us
From a past so long ago
That to fathom them is a test.

But, be they the narrowest,
Most piercing of insights,
Or the broadest
Warmest of floods imaginable,
Gather in the light as it comes.
Tend it,
Burnish your day whilst you can.

For, in all the spaces in between,
See how the devil gapes...
And what space he has to do his mischief!

The time to consolidate such moments
Often hangs by a thread,
When there are so many in the world
That might seek to swallow such blessings whole
And smother them in darkness.
Drown them in their own constant,
But clever discrimination
Of selfish need, greed and ambition
That instead demands a foil,
A litany of vacuous praise, of reassurance,
A monument, a Godhead even!

What fools...

So much beauty
Slaughtered needlessly
On the altar of achievement.
And for what?
When, beyond all this vanity,
There are so many more powerful hinges
Into the graceful and the divine.

On the high road of life
So many false turns,
So many missed opportunities.

Not stolen from us
By any illusion of cruel fate
Or malign third party,
Wasted only by lethargy
And an appetite for self indulgence.

This much we can all divine
And be sure of.

Shelter from this truth,
Seek shallow comfort
For as long as you chose...
But, however rich or poor,
However downcast or mighty,
There is nowhere to hide.

No excuses left
For either hopelessness or self pity,
When it is the most humble
And yet luminous amongst us
That live and feel this axis the most.

Truly a bequest to all.
And one that will wait
For each one of us forever,
If it needs to.

Knowing that with the will,
With no more than constancy
And a good heart,
There is so much space for grace,
So many possibilities,
So much further to go.

And squander this gift,
As we often do,
Ultimately not one amongst us
Will ever be denied that,
The glimmer of a chance to shine.

The perpetual riddle of life.

How a host of individual
Spiritual entities
Can be seemingly cast carelessly adrift
On some vast, ancient sea of neural messages
That is the collective unconscious.

Perhaps though,
Even when considered all together,
We are no more than an impulse,
A shiver in the breeze,
The merest hint of presence
In an echo of loneliness.

All unconsciously following
A starlit scatter trail of dreams
That one day might lead us
To a glorious point of transformation,
When the best of our psyches
Will fuse together like a thunderbolt.

Much as how long, long ago,
Just one piercing blow
From a Mayan tomahawk
Could smash a single skull asunder.
And thus make our world anew,
Shower it with enlightenment never ending.

Be you a babe in arms,
Newly flush with life,
An infant excited,
A lover who has never felt more alive.

However young and fresh faced,
However delighted, dulled or weary,
The experience of age is in your every move,
Your every thought, your every instinct,
Each breath you take.

Imagine the storyboard of your life.
The inspirations and ecstasies,
The struggles and despair
And, just for a moment,
Gaze back and see a fluid pattern.
How the river of your life has twisted and turned
How it has gathered, coalesced
And how it nudges you still,
How it eases you gently forward.

Like the hands of the clock that shift so softly,
Though we can't quite discern it,
Notice how your own golden harvest piles up,
And with it its tithe, both in its glory
And ultimately its tax upon you for life's bequest.

Remember that everyday you still awake,
With good fortune and opportunity,
To the gathering warmth of a new day.

With joy in your heart,
Everyday can be extraordinary
And ripe,
Like a flower burst,
If the will is there.

For sure, on some days,
Fate may seem heartless,
As if acting with intent to interfere,
To punish, or to twist you away
From where you think you want to be.

But there are surprises.

Fresh hope, new life
Sometimes finds its breath
In just such a clash of expectation.
And, as stories of destinies retold
Often remind us,
Even in a cruel coming together
Of opposing forces,
Something rare and beautiful,
Something precious can emerge.

Something new born.
Duly forged, fused
Within what frequently appears,
From the outset, at least,
To be a haphazard or ill-judged coupling,
Of whose choosing I'm not sure?

For such matters of conception
Remain shrouded in mystery,
As they should be.

Auspicious, certainly!

And the bonus is
That there is therefore
No burden of responsibility,
No pedestal for us to fall from,
Other than accepting that,
On the canvas of life,
Every sweep of the brush matters,
Counts for something...

And so it falls to us
To do no more than respond,
To confirm significance.
And this, believe me,
Whatever our gender or strength,
We can all manage
With unique shades of brilliance,
A blooming of our own.

Just as, in perfect symmetry,
The emerging budded plant
Opens wide, toward the sun
And a stiff phallus will forever beg
For its home, for its comfort,
Its release,
Deep into a soft inner refuge
So that it may speak, discharge itself.

Thus, or so it seems,
Does the light need only our trust
And, of course, the darkness
To work its eternal alchemy.

Life collects, pools around you.
It paints its highlights,
Nothing there you can destroy
Or begin again.

Calm in aquamarine beauty,
Barely a hint of surf's snowy trim.
Today the sea is out
But will come again.

For the moment,
On the beach,
My love and I,
Naked and blissful as can be.

In the soft, sun baked sand
History between my toes.

Sense how
Even the smooth stones ache
With stories of their own
In the shuddering light of day.

When in love or inspired,
An eternal kiss from the divine
Awaits us all.

Just as the frostiest of old maids
Secretly longs to tremble
With excitement in her bed,
One more time.
Or the pained young lover
Pitifully nurses a wound
That renders their heart homeless,
Mourning the loss of romance
Seemingly gone forever.
The truth is
Nothing that truly matters
Can ever evaporate,
Be excised,
Burnt out of your soul.

And however ready
We may or may not be,
At any stage in our life,
There will always be the chance
To reclaim our essence,
The shape we call our own.

For, once spun,
The silken thread of all our aspirations
Remains intact,
It can never be broken.
And, with courage, even a trail of tears
Will always lead us back
To where our fractured heart longs to be.

So that, just as the wise old Shoguns
Chose to,
With their most precious of porcelain vessels,
We too can repair our cracks with gold
And glow again.
Crazed by life,
More beautiful than ever before.

Inside every single,
Obdurate, intractable skull
Is an entire universe humming,
Every bit as vast as the heavens above,
From whence we all came.

And with that realisation
Comes a power
That can melt tyranny itself,
Lay waste any dictator's cannon.

And all this played out
Within a prescribed arena,
Forever licensed to allow us full rein.

Albeit that we remain bound
To a narrative
That sometimes still needs
To remind us of our mortality,
And in so doing,
Will punish and wound,
Seemingly without care or remorse.

But be not afeared.
Wear any such scars well,
Knowing that,
For every moment of suffering,
Others will arrive
That will instead pierce you with joy.

Open the doors of your heart and they will come...

And for every cruel arrow,
Sweet caresses of delirium also
To nourish your soul.

In the shadows of my life
I spy something still askew.

On a grey sombre winter's afternoon,
The sound of stillness
Penetrates space
To highlight what's missing.

In a corner though,
Soft pastel energy
Breathes and glows still,
Its perfection somehow more obvious
In the muted light.
As if the gentlest of reminders
To dare to love more.

To recapture bliss and rapture,
That sense of clashing golden symbols,
Of sparking chimes in the ether.

Too often we choose instead
To become lulled,
To forget life shrinks or expands
In relation to courage showed,
Becalmed by the risk of pain or loss
And outcomes that can never be certain.

And, until something stirs,
Who or what gives you that tug,
I wonder?

A summons that beckons you upwards again,
Like an ocean diver ascendant,
Bursting to the surface,
Back into the clear blue skies
And bright yellow light,
The frothing oxygen of hope and exhilaration.

This is the gilded spiral
Of longings within.
Our very own cathedral
That points persistently to heaven.

How precious then the gloom
Beneath these vaulted spires,
And, within such confines,
The needs and wounds
That first find time there
To open us up,
Then lift us homeward again.

For Rebecca

Brave,
Or maybe not?
Needs must...
Fausse mesure
Circumstance toys with us all,
I'm afraid.

Some may say it's fate's cruel hand,
A toss of the dice:
'Born to whom, exposed to what...'

Safe?
Or maybe instead
Endowed with a hungry soul
That's been enchanted to risk too much.

Loved?
Or then again perhaps
Abandoned, exploited,
Burnt by the hollow pain of others.
And then left alone,
With a need to heal,
To escape such abject despair.

Jagged crevices most will never see
Or can even imagine.

Who, if anyone, is lucky then?
I'm not so sure...

Those charmed enough
To sail through life's voyages
Woundless, intact?
Or those who were once staggering,
Bleeding,
Damaged and lost,
Who have somehow found the way back
To their own angel within...

For, in the harshest
Most constricted of circumstance,
And uniquely so,
Do the most precious of all jewels come into being.

Treasure forever is what we know this to be.

So to have been where you have been
And to still have joy,
Dazzling in your heart,
Now there's a thing to make the whole world smile.

If you can be,
Be entirely naked - as one to another.
Not just in your body,
But surrender also
Every close kept need,
Your fears, all that you hold dear...

And, in so doing,
Together conjure something delightful,
Pursue it to a crescendo
And in the calmness that follows,
Almost by accident,
You will have stumbled on the immeasurable.

As if a thousand nights of passion,
Of ecstasy, of insight and elevation
Have been scooped up, there and then,
To be kept forever in your soul.

I promise you
This is so much more
Than mortal love God given,
This is the religion
Of elevated experience,
Of true sanctity,
Long striven for, hard won...

And with this triumph
Comes a spiritual gateway,
Rarely even glimpsed,
Triggered to open only to such discovery,
When joy and humility finally bubble up
Simultaneously
To stain the day eternal in their glorious hue.

And, once achieved,
Should the levy of age,
The passing of years
Ever tempt you to doubt it,
Just pause for a moment and feel
How such sweet pivots in time
Remembered,
Ripen still, even in solitude.
Like fabulous guests
Re-visiting a sun-lit porch
That has waited seemingly forever
To welcome them home again.

For me it's easier to embrace, I guess.
Long wedded to the quest
And not just some otherwise busy,
Preoccupied visitor
Indifferently passing through.

But I suppose we are all
Writers of our own lives,
Are we not?

How much better - joy laden
The story is then,
If one remains
Free enough in your spirit
To always find some time at least,
To be as a child would be.

Able to hone in, to find the pulse
Of whatever small excitements,
Opportunities, otherwise easily missed,
That life still so often puts our way.

Believe me,
To catch and plant them all
Would soon fill your open heart
To bursting point,
If you were ever that artful.

For, as adulthood takes hold,
Poised
And seductively accomplished
As it often may well be,
How barren is the vessel
That has no seed left within.

Ambition's the thing,
For sure.
Desires irrevocably ignited
By creative resonance.

A wish to travel that same path,
To follow a tracer line
Of those that came before you,
In sporadic explosions
Of piercing self expression
And insight,
Fierce splintering beauty
Fired out into the darkness.

And even when life
Is as its stillest,
Most becalmed,
Their energised presence lingers
And haunts us still,
Like mysterious smoky lanterns
In the circling mists of uncertainty
They chose to explore.

Clues embedded
In swaying shadows
And curious shapes of thought
Left behind,
A stream of primal voices
Whispering in the breeze of your heart
To urge you on.

As an artist,
This is about the places
You are prepared to take your soul to.

Go in far and deep enough,
As most are too afeard to,
Then there are, of course,
Rich and fabulous seams of treasure
To mine,
Bejewelled slivers of which
You can then bring back
To the surface of life
For others to see and feel,
As if theirs.
To gaze and wonder at ...

Anchored as you are to a destiny,
Which is not nearly so temporary
As all you experience,
It is what it is, this impulse still to act.

Knowing for sure that
Some things are more precious
Because they don't last forever.

Sometimes, caught in the thrall,
There's no option
But to just stand and gape in amazement
At what you can discover,
And all that has still somehow
Found its way back to you.

For here you are,
At a fixed point
On a grid of possibilities
That is the architecture
Of happiness itself.

Knowing that, at any one time,
It is only for you and you alone,
To decide to stay or move on,
To pause, or to reach out
And clasp something new
Close to your heart,
Wedded as we are, quite rightly,
To an ambition to luxuriate fully
In life's rich promise.

And the truth is you are indeed
As wonderfully and perilously free
As this suggests.

All this and more you may taste
And explore,
With the best of intentions
And, as if none of it will leave
Even a fleck upon you!

Knowing all the while,
Of course,
This is not really
How the story runs.

Give not honestly of yourself,
And you will corrode the core
Of much that matters.
Shine true instead
And you may well linger
In the light of love,
Maybe even longer
Than you feel you have a right to.

And of course
There's so much in between,
Muddled by prescribed faith,
Morality
And the ever shifting tolerances
Of others that will hasten to judge
Or condemn you.

No reliable arbiter of choices
Before you then,
Save your own inner voice,
Should you take care to listen.

But surely
As just one seeker
Of souls harmony,
Netted but never quite landed
In this world,
To catch even one glistening moment
Of sweet release,
As full, as fine, as pure
As ever could be hoped for,
Would be bounty sufficient to last a lifetime?

Now there's the rub...

Be as audacious
As you wish.
By all means look to the heavens.

But, as you labour so
In this glorious snare,
Take care to tend to the wounds
Of your enthusiasm.

Because it's not till it's broken and bust,
Genuinely beaten up,
That you realise just how fluid,
How soft and aching,
How finite a liquid chamber
Any human being is,
Given its every flush of hope
And inspiration,
Its residue of angst and despair.

The wonder, the sheer scale
Of its emotional range
And yet, as if to confound us all,
Its raw and visceral vulnerability.

Yes indeed,
What an extraordinarily delicate
And tender thing it is we have here.

For less than a moment
In our incessantly indifferent world,
One raging soul's crazy dances,
Like a drunken butterfly,
Painting the day fitfully
With its own show of colour,
In search of the sun.

For Natalie

However you may shine,
Infection is everywhere
And it's a nonsense.

Look at what they can hang before us.
The sordid greed of the world itself,
Like shroud bearers in the Plague,
And grubbily persistent too,
As if they have no shame,
Nor right it seems
To share with us
The blessed light of the day.

Interwoven with selfish desires
To be ashamed of,
It's the cold wind of fear though
That sometimes calls you to them.

After all, your life in this circus
Has already been quite a procession,
Stretching back into the distance
To precipitate this point.

A long line of enquiry
Inevitably riddled with mistakes.

Hurting as you may be
Right now,
What a wonderful thing it is
Not to be alone.

This ashen cloth
Won't ever quite leave me be either,
Living as I do on a prayer.

But, as my eyes lift again
To the world,
I can at least be with you.

Your body, your spirit
Healing like warm stones,
Sourcing and soothing the exhaustion
In my soul,
So I can fall back skyward,
Safe in your arms,
And survive to dream again.

You know how it is.
After all, in this life at least,
Our fate is rarely epic.

Maybe just as well,
Impervious heroes we are not...

No more than porous
Flesh and blood,
Blessed with all the vagaries
That accompany that sometime glorious
And often uneasy state,
Given our need to absorb,
To recover
From whatever comes our way,
For the journey ahead is a long one.

All this a pageant of life
Far easier to observe
In others, of course.

And because of that
It's so easy sometimes
Yourself
To just slide away,
To melt, oh so slowly
And unnoticed,
Into some long yawning drift
To nowhere left at all,
Where real joy might still be shining.

Alive, but as if lost
To any hope of rescue or rejuvenation.

That is till inner needs conjure,
As if in spite of you,
The alchemy of unexpected experience
Or chance encounter with a kindred spirit,
The kindness of strangers maybe?
Any of which might touch and re-ignite
Something precious within.

Mislaid flame of tender emotions
Rekindled.

And with this comes a sudden rush
Of warmth and validation
In the ensuing embrace,
The consequent smile,
The sigh of insight,
Or the tear that falls afresh.
As we stumble upon a brief moment
Of illuminated reflection
That, as if gifted,
Blesses and unburdens everything.
And you are an orphan to your soul
No more.

In memory of Anthony Aikman

As the wisest of scholars
Have always known,
It remains stubbornly unfathomable
Just how far inspiration can take you.

So best not to risk extinguishing
Possibilities of insight,
That sometimes
Only the opportunity of reflection
And simple stasis can bring.

For it's never quite what's garnered
Or understood
But rather, what you feel inside,
That conditions your chances.
All the rest is no more than fool's gold
That will choke you at your greediest.

However foolish one could ever be,
Fresh opportunities will always remain.
So what is time to even tempt you
To act in any way premature,
When late really doesn't exist,
It is nowhere at all...

And even when you feel
You haven't moved any closer
To where your heart truly hungers to be,
That's precisely the time
When it's hardest of all to see
That its desire
That often gets in the way the most.

For there are always easier,
More immediately rewarding paths
To chose, ahead of others
That genuinely hold the key.
And it's difficult to do anything other
Than stay with the familiar,
Given all you've acquired
And assembled
Progressively around you.

Inevitable too that the body,
With all its innate
And transitory desires,
Will always fail
Whilst the soul never will.

Waiting patiently, as it does,
Till the frail chamber of your being
Is free at last of clutter
And the cravings of an instinct,
That so rabidly collects totems
Alluding to permanence
Falsely claimed, never quite captured.

But this is life as it truly is, my friend...

And even if you were ever
To achieve a state of being
Far beyond the dreams of avarice,
Of any mortal imagination,
It all comes to nought in the end.

So look how foolishly we believe
Our lives to be empty – but not so,
Till clotted with greed and lusts
That satisfy but for a moment,
Before we inevitably ache for more.

Of course,
This is a madness of sorts.
Knowing that,
Whatever we lay claim to,
Death will always burst through in the end.
And thereby become
Every bit the monster we make it.

After all, what worse a curse
To wish on your enemies
Than the cravings and desires
Of self importance realised.

And for even the enlightened ones
Amongst us, what use then
The most beautiful of instruments?
If you lack the skill to play
(And like an angel too!)
But only if with the humility
Required to even begin...

From pauper to thief,
From peasant to monarch,
Such a chance is granted to us all,
Be we humble enough to see it.

So proceed generously,
Measure out a little of this
And a little of that, along the way.
And find out slowly
What it takes to make you soul sing.

If you can,
Be brave enough to never yearn
For that you cannot hold close
In your heart forever.
Tread lightly, cherish compassion
And live in the moment without fear.

For IO

Sharp and attuned,
Blessed with the greatest gift of all
- Compassion,
Some are destined to tell stories
That show us the way
To where we long to be.

Some say life's a mystery.
Others, forever young at heart,
May disagree.

There's absolutely no quandary
There, they say...
Just feel the light
And let your heart warm,
Till all and every possibility
Of hurt and doubt
Simply melts away.

So I share your tears, Joanna.
Tears of joy, of certainty,
Of longings too,
Of when we all will be as one
In light never ending.

You and I,
We have never met face to face.
But believe me,
I still smile nevertheless,
Each time I think of you.

Knowing that you, like me,
Feel the celestial gravity
In your soul,
Feel the stars ache kindly,
As they wait patiently
For us.

What became of you, my love?

The years have flown by...

The distance between us though,
Moulded,
Shaped by life's experience,
Is a kind one.
Perhaps always knowing more
Than we ever did then
At our most youthful and resplendent.

Wow!
We had a time, didn't we?
And it lingers still like fire burn,
Like lamp light in my being.

So just imagine
At this very moment,
Somewhere in the world,
Two lovers are busy at play,
Ecstatic,
Aflame for the very first time.

Think of that
And let your heart stir again
So gloriously,
As it did once before.

For Maureen

Whatever joys come our way,
The road ahead will be a hard one.
Your kinship though is precious,
Like sweet molasses,
Fuel for my journey.

Sometimes returning,
Battered and bruised I admit,
My basket full of
Fresh hewn promises,
Chiselled out and polished in hope.

And with all my dreams too
Of what could come true,
Of what my labours long to proffer you.

You know I give you my love, as best I can.

Together we live to the point of tears,
I wouldn't want it any other way.

Such things happen.
And, for a time,
Under their shrivelled cowl
There's little else we can do.

Never sadder or more downcast
Than when bereaved, deserted,
Damaged, neglected.

And however deep we delve
For speedy comfort,
For reassurance
That we cannot help but yearn for,
When random tragedy
Or the cold cruelty of others
Tarnish the day,
There can be none.

Unless you possess
The zinc heart of a zealot,
Born of the brutalities of others,
There are answers though.
Despite the awful hazards
That, in living,
We have no choice but to embrace.

How unspeakably sad that
However pure, however cherished
And safe in times past,
Something, anything, anyone
Still here with us
Can still be spoilt and ruined so,
When left prey to circumstance
And the callous whims
Of those already lost in the darkness.

Legacy though,
Like the light of love
In any infant's eye,
Remains impervious
To any such violation,
Seeding aspirations that live on.

Inspiration to rise above
A mass of malignant possibilities
And, in so doing, remind each other of
Just what the human spirit is capable of.

There may well be times in your life
When you lose sight of your soul.
But, trust me, it can always see you...

A hallowed frequency within
That, even in your darkest hour,
You can always turn to.
Knowing that,
When the tortures of self doubt
And the bitterest of all tears
Are in your eyes,
This choice remains forever yours.

Favoured,
Doted on or not,
We are all born
With a bewilderment of choices.
But, of course,
Remain far less certain of purpose,
Till becalmed enough to notice
What's pregnant in our soul.

And thus, in such a way,
Is our fate summoned,
As if prescient, to play its part.

All this must rise up
And still come from within though,
Just as a sickness
Can often be the healer
To free you from disease,
So let it flow through you
Like warm summer sunlight on your limbs.

Welcome that risk.
Let life lead you
And answer its call truthfully,
Without recourse
To the pernicious clatter
Of frigid moral reinforcement
That only wastes your time,
In a world where, trust me,
To appease your own timidity
Is the most common error of all.

Far better this,
The heat of genesis,
Than freezing for a lifetime
And then suddenly finding yourself
Nowhere at all. Your race run
And with no-one left to share
Your deepest innermost hopes,
Your hunger for bliss,
Your yearning to belong.

The only reward for reticence
Being an empty dark space
And a rush of panicked terror
To fill that void
Before the circle of death closes in.

So, for every precious little moment
That ever graces to visit you,
Take special care to embrace
And capture its cachet there and then.

For the instant it lives and breathes
And is there to savour and polish so,
Especially with those you love
Close beside you,
Then that is true happiness, my friend.
And it shines on forever...

Life proceeds for us all,
Knowing that anything
That might make the world
Sit up and take notice,
Has little to do with
Any notion of innate talent
That the foolish
Might rush to foist upon you.

Some recognition at least
In favour of persistent endeavour
To realise the grit in the oyster,
The very guts
Of all you might dare to dream
To be.

So press on with fresh hope
And, upon your journey,
Keep an eye out for those
We should all learn to value.
Our prophets, our guides,
Too many to count,
Would that we knew it...

See how they come and go
And in many guises too,
Some welcome, some not so,
Along the way.

Many remaining
Stubbornly incognito
Till they have long since
Played their part
And are no more,
Oft as innocent and unknowing
As any
Caught in this whirlpool of existence.

Driven by powers
Beyond their own knowing,
They scatter seeds before us.
Precious scraps of insight,
Glimpses of promises
To keep the song birds
In our heart coming back.
And all planted with a purpose,
To seek to limit regret
Not to have done more
With the chances we've been given.

So should we always look
To honour them
With the light we give back.

Still and stopped
As you may well
Sometimes have to be,
By all means, welcome belief
And inspiration,
Whenever it pays you a call.

Triggers towards something
Gleaming and rare perhaps?

Tempting isn't it though
To rush to act?
As if we are all no more
Than shallow juveniles,
Foolishly marooned
On some capricious isle,
Some temporary outcrop
In time and space,
Especially when to be human
Is seemingly
Such an arbitrary experience.

And as for myself,
A surprise!

Looking back now,
I can see how my whole future,
My entire destiny,
Lay, all the while beside me,
As I slept, warm and soundly,
Like some fat snake in summer
Basking on a stony coastal path.

Even then,
There was a sense of belonging...
Paradise is no whim.
It takes time and trust,
You see.

A need to pause, to rest.

It's at times like these
That I best notice
A bewilderment of gifts,
Treasures I never knew I had.

Just one long look out at the world
Any sunlit morning
Excites me so,
Makes my heart ache.
Sometimes gets me thinking
I have woken somewhere else,
Somewhere new and exotic,
Exquisitely perfumed.

How revealing is that?

And so it means what it means,
This need to confess
That, for all our flailing around,
For all our yearnings
And our heart aches,
We barely scratch the surface
Of something so simple.

And therefore can be
Caught so unawares...

Climb too enthusiastically
Into a mirror of the self
And you may never get out,
Never escape the greedy maze
Of its seductive stare.

For myself, I understand
I simply have to be
And give, as best I can.
And then just leave.

Complicit in lingering too long?
I hope not...

Far better to focus instead
On establishing a warmth
And light within,
That begins to stir
Your very own story.
Then, at whatever point in your life,
You have a way forward,
A purpose to begin.

Follow its lead,
Treasure wherever it takes you,
Make of it what you will.
And when the heat
Of its giddy energy
Starts to fade,
Then you know
Your time may be running short.

Once in a while,
Along the way,
By all means pause
To consider your situation,
If you must!
Like the most delicate of cautious spiders
That sometime
Might still think it necessary to flee
Or to stop and fight,
To quarrel,
To consume or be consumed...

Your fate though
Is not nearly as tentative
Or parlous as this.

For, along the oft fearful
And meandering trail,
The miasm of life,
Your hallowed soul within
Still offers you clear direction
And fragrant sanctuary.

Sacred space in which
To distil, like amber,
The best of your love.
And forgives you also
For mistakes of the heart
And nostalgia for moments gone,
But not forgotten...

The best of times
When you shone as you should.

The true harvest here
Is inestimable,
Endless gilded web
It radiates forever.

Ripples and tremors of light,
You may never see their end...

As we set off on our journey,
Brittle circumstance...

Whatever predispositions
Or genetic triggers,
Nothing is set in stone.

After all, however sedulous,
Mere coincidence and false trails,
There to be misappropriated,
Are found all too easily.
And believe me they can play tricks
The devil himself would be proud of...

Before us all then
Is a rolling scroll of contours,
An etched landscape
Far better viewed
At one step removed.
And not close to,
As we find to our cost.
But meditatively from a distance,
So inherent prospects
Can be seen for what they truly are.

After all,
Such internal natures,
Bubbling away beneath the surface,
Are fiercely strong
Are they not?

Mighty forces indeed,
Above which
To set forth on such adventures,
And where it falls to us all
To decide who or what we bestow
Our energies, our heart's yearning,
The very best of our honour upon.

Trusting that nothing
Will get in the way of that truth.

So imagine, if you will,
Summoning up
All the faith
You could ever possibly have,
There on the leash
And then letting it out incrementally,
Like some rushing stallion
Who chases the sun on the horizon,
In pursuit of incandescence.

And thus is integrity's pathway
Befittingly fuelled and illuminated
By such fire and passion,
And as if always meant to be...

As the years slip by...
For every blissful balmy day,
That once, as a child,
Seemed so endless...
Now there's a pace
And a harshness
In the weather
That sometimes feels like
It was never there before.

And to think that
Every crease
In this kind landscape of ours
Was once a vibrant river of sorts,
Even if it was only the briefest,
Most ancient of glacial rushes
That caused the first scar.

And so it is also
On the terrain of the soul,
Where sprites can dance
So freely,
The dice are rolled
And energy bends time,
Making daylight of passion.

Though given
All this froth and ferment,
Perhaps discernment of risk
Is a curse?
Or maybe it's a blessing?

For much as it may be
An uncomfortable truth,
That most of us
Would far rather renounce,
Together we all live every moment
On the very brink;
The razor's edge
Of ecstasy or disaster.
But rarely meet either, of course...

That goes with the ticket though,
Doesn't it?
The price of admission to so much:
The chance of sunlight on our skin,
As well as the sweet, sweet air
We suck into our lungs to cry.

Room to stretch, to grow, to dream...

Too often, along the way,
Persuasive hope
Loses its sway it seems.
For there's nothing so sad
As ordinary folk content,
Their dreams over,
Smothered...

Nevertheless, despite the vagaries
Of any such humdrum tale,
Whatever you briefly dared to dream,
Whoever you might
Have once claimed to be,
You can't go on
Denying yourself forever.

And so,
When your heart hits a note,
When you glimpse yourself
In the sky again,
Distant echoes...
Can you trust what you feel?

Try to believe though,
Knowing that the need for fear
And control
Are both such eager
And complicit partners in crime.

So relinquish them both
And, on a truly glad day,
Then will come the light,
Arrowed supreme to your heart.

If someone, anyone
Ever loved you
They never leave you entirely.

In the aftermath of their loss
Though,
Hard not to avoid
Desperate attempts
To conjure ill-judged conclusions
From such a fracture.

See how we scurry
In the darkness of our pain
To usurp, to filch the light,
Anything to try and bandage the soul!
Picking up the shards of belonging,
To piece together again
Before we imagine it's too late.

Almost frantic,
Here we are busily
Losing our religion,
When we almost had it all.

So much for generosity and gratitude,
Now seemingly savaged away
By such a schism.

For what are we,
When stripped and laid bare
By such setbacks,
If not mere grotesques?

Without light and faith,
Just a telling echo of the reptile's tail
And the spike in the rib cage
That once, eons ago,
Was sorely needed to survive
Much harsher, less cosmetic times.

Curious and troublesome,
We certainly still are...

Perhaps then
No more than temporary anomalies,
Caged to suffer
For little more than a moment
In this world?

But once snared,
Surely hooked forever...
After all,
Should you dare to look
Into the endless abyss
It stares straight back at you.

I'm no Cassandra,
But, mere mortals such as we are,
This is our life's bequest:
Hungry for meaning
That's storm laden,
And, trust me, it's all coming,
Rolling in, it's on the way...

So take comfort from knowing
That to have once been so desperate,
So low,
Pilloried by fate and fellow alike;
And then magically,
As if from nowhere
And in answer to prayer,
To be blessed with joy,
Then this is truly how it has to be.

Each of us orphans
On this dizzy sphere,
Initially cast adrift
Without a mooring point.

Even as infants,
We hunt intuitively
On the surface
Of the kind natural world,
That immediately enfolds us,
For divine connection
And it offers us just that,
Even if only fleetingly.

Weak as we are,
It's not always possible
To hold station for long enough
To heal as we should.
But look how,
With all our hungers,
Our needs stretched
On the steely breeze of existence,
We do so love to feel
The warmth of safe harbour
Whenever we find it.

Here we can nuzzle,
Nestle for a while,
And feel safe enough
To open ourselves up,
As we need to...
In search of the key
To trials and experiences
That will make us whole again.

Summoning up the compassion
To share the pain of others,
Or fearlessly becoming
The fiercest of lovers perhaps?

And how I long
For that abandonment again
More than anything else,
And the opportunity it offers,
With our gift of self,
To rouse something eternal
In the ascendant,
Impervious to all peril or decay.

A luminous shape
To forever call our own.

For sure
Death comes to us all.

Perhaps then,
As our time approaches
And a sense of settlement
Comes upon us,
We must do our best
To bear witness.

After all, we all start
And finish this journey
As little more than hapless children,
And life therefore
Is always a victory of sorts.

So, as you leave, smile
And light a single candle
In the darkness anyway.

Along the way,
On this excursion of ours,
There is a need for measure,
An epicurean ability
Without which
The whole cavalcade
Is rendered no more than
A senseless orgy of beasts.
A greedy manic rush,
From room to room,
In the castle of your dreams.

So, each and every time
You are so visited,
Slowed and diverted
By selfless light and radiance,
Be sure to pause
And treat this happenstance
As the passing charm that it is.

Like the most precious
Of all hostages to keep safe,
To clasp close to your heart,
As you would a lover's jewel.
To burnish
For just as long you can,
Before fate's temporal denouement
Creeps in
And such joy is no more...

For these fabled moments
Often melt away all too soon,
As if stolen from your soul,
Slipping through your fingers
Just as easily and prettily
As they were once found,
So fortuitously,
Like sparkling garnets in a stream
On the moated riverbed of life.

And, as any seeker,
However courageous,
Knows only too well,
An element of mishap
Is sometimes inevitable.
For the very capriciousness
Of the process is itself a mirror,
A key definer of the quality
Of the chances you are given.

And despite
Any such flux in fortune,
A material depth,
Not present before,
Gradually accrues,
As your burgeoning life,
With all its strands,
Its threads pulling together,
Slowly becomes
A marvellously rich book,
Steadily gathering folios and meaning.

So try your best
Neither to fret,
Nor be too ambitious
To ever notice such slips,
Because unexpected magic
Can often happen too,
Between such pages,
When, even briefly,
Disparate energies come together
That have never been aligned before.

And so bound,
Is the world illuminated,
Changed forever in an instant...

However comfortable a perch
You may eventually stumble upon,
Always remember your story.
For hazards are everywhere
And no one, however charmed,
Is immune to suffering.

But like the starving beggar,
Who tears at discarded dirty bread
To eat,
And who is so near the precipice
He can almost hear himself living,
Life must always go on.

Remembering that,
Whether we imagine it to be so,
Or not,
We are all the same.
No less frail than one another.

Ultimately any individual
Determines far less
Than we imagine,
Driven by imperatives
That agitate our responsibilities,
Both for ourselves and others.

And, however we might chose
To dress it up,
The warmth of the passing sunlight,
We are given,
Will always eventually be chased down,
Till our torn hope
Competes with fading dreams.

So, even given the moments
When we shone as we should,
Such will be our eventual
And oft regretful points of departure,
On a trajectory of life
Where nothing,
However tragic,
Is ever meaningless or accidental.

Therefore we all
Must do our very best
To roll away the stones,
Conspiratorial partners on our excursion,
Fearing not...
Knowing that death,
Like some sacred iridescent cloth,
Sweeps all before it.
And in so doing,
Releases all haunting memories
Of what we once were
Into light everlasting.

A need for connection,
Attachment.
Drawn in, enchanted by
Resonances with nature
And the kinship of others,
With beauty
Forged by heart's endeavour.

And so should we
Always aspire to polish
Such precious attainment
With love,
A blessed friction of sorts
That allows us
To birth our night into day
And bathe it clean,
So that beloved things can glow
Together in a litter of light.

We are anything but finite
Or alone!
After all the petals of proof
Are here in our hearts,
Are they not?

And however deflated
We might sometimes be,
Either by our own frailties
Or the cruelty of others,
- Inviolate -
At the core of our being,
The very prism
Of sanctity and self remains.

And latent there,
The quick silvered opportunity
Of redemption,
To become enchanted again.

Sublime moments refracted,
Even if only for seconds,
Caught forever in your soul.

Mere beasts we once were,
So there must be an element of bravado
To dare to even conceive
Of any alternative idyll.

For amidst the haunting chaos
Of what we might dream
For ourselves,
Poisoned splendour
And hollow vanity await,
Like swollen vipers,
To bite
If ambition is ever misplaced.

Growing slowly together
Towards love though,
Is undeniably a tender sweet truth.

Feelings and expressions
Carefully bottled
And decanted with certainty,
Till fused
With the compliant surrender
Of sudden penetration needed
To share one's stake in being alive.

Imagine
Just what has been absorbed
In that one savage moment.

How poetic then that
The road to a bloodied birth
Has thus been prompted,
So that another psyche altogether
Might too take its chances.

And all the while
There is a discernable presence
It seems, just watching...
That knows this
To be a ceaseless tide
Of frail hope,
That swells and swells
And will, in time,
Ebb away within you.

Such is the circle of life,
A rush of blood
In the spiritual stir of the world
That gives us our passion,
Our noble impetus.

And so, for as long
As my veins still pulse,
I promise to love as best I can.
I will strive and suffer
To change the course of things.

For Isla

You are wonderful,
Diamond lit.

And every time I look at you,
I see such a wide open soul
Already seemingly
At perfect peace with the world,
Where you landed not so long ago,
Soft and starlit,
Like an enchanted feather in the night.

For me, the simple
But exquisitely tender feeling
You engender in my heart
Is brilliant, beyond all expectation...

And whilst it's true
You may, as yet,
Still be so young and new,
All I have learnt
On my much longer visitation so far,
Tells me that times spent with you
Are destined to be
Some of the truest of my life.

How lucky I am then
To have found you
Circuitously in my life.
And, whatever now lies ahead
For us both,
Never stop trusting
That the joy in your gentle soul
Is something I will carry
On my way forever...

So, please always remember
To smile for me,
Especially when I've gone.
And you are still here,
Dancing your dance
And laughing away,
As you always seem to do...

Graced with the chance to be here,
Even if only fleetingly,
Embrace whatever comes your way
And, in so doing,
However enchanting
Any treasures you uncover
Might be,
Their loss should never be your concern.

In this matter
Make your heart your queen
And follow her as faithfully
And bravely as you are able,
Just as swelling fruit
Hurries towards its own sweetness,
Shine whilst you can,
Without fear,
For nothing is as inevitable
As it seems here.
No, not even the fissures
Of loss and decay
We are oft led to expect
In this temporal world.

For whilst we fuss and fudge
The lines we are given,
Above, below and all around us,
Lingers the energy of countless others
Who already know for sure
That, just as it was long, long ago,
When they first found themselves
Enraptured,
So it is for them, again and again...
And now with only a dark empty hollow,
A feeble space of earth left in between.

Such is true joy's absolute certainty,
Its slow lit fuse that burns holes
In the shabby shroud of death forever.

Captive

We certainly are not.

Life, if we wish it to be,
Being nought
But some loose masquerade.

And within this conceit,
This mannered dance,
The freedom to lay a multitude
Of false trails,
To adopt such an array of guises,
Even the simplest of souls
Could easily become dizzy
With the choices before them.

See how so many pose and preen
In the seething ferment of the world.

And how seduced they are,
To the extent
It becomes almost comic.
After all, to make some impact,
No more than a little boldness
Is required
And greedily gathering
All the blooms for yourself
Always comes easily enough.

For sure
You are allowed to do that,
My friend!
So go ahead if you must...

But what does that ever achieve
Other than a soul, left drowning
In the eager swash of self indulgence.

And so it is,
When you have lost your way.

A howling emptiness
And dignity shredded for what?
When something entirely different
And more generously spirited
Is forever within your grasp.

Prudent it seems then
To cling on elsewhere,
Given that, however giddy
The day may have seemed,
When we are alone and becalmed
In the dark of night,
The plain, unvarnished truth
Is never that far away.

And, like it or not,
That gnawing sense
Of purposelessness
Will always return,
Again and again,
In waves, to haunt us...
To hold us all to account
And, one day, hopefully
To set us free.

Knowing that
Nothing or no one
Could ever contain our spirit,
If we but learn to embrace
Who we truly are.

Anna Karenina to her lover, Count Vronsky

Laid bare,
Ripped open
By the sheer joy
We allowed ourselves to share,
I sensed then
This had to be the beginning
Of the end of everything.

For all I have left for you now
My love,
Is my steady heart,
My humble happiness.

And so, damned and blessed
In equal measure,
Such is the cycle of romance,
Or so it seems...

Capricious, frail
And yet, at times, so wondrous
And all encompassing.

Yet now I can see so clearly
How, when the rose first opens,
Its thorny stock stiff and fit to burst,
Such divine and fevered feelings
Are released in a perfumed crescendo
That, from that day on,
Can never be quite as sweet again.

Maybe better this though
Than fidelity?
Some persistent fervour
That, even in its noble rawness
And good intent,
The world can spoil so easily...
And one day, no doubt,
Would have only succeeded
In choking itself.

When it comes to passion,
We might as well be beasts, it seems.
Though, trust me,
I would not have believed it to be so then.

But Oh,
To have lived such a dream
And cruelly to still be here now,
Full bloodied,
Feeling the warmth of the sun
When, no doubt, you are with another.

So now it has to be farewell!

The truth is I will never stop loving you
And am therefore irretrievably lost...
And that, my darling,
Even in death,
Has no matter of reason within it
I can be forgiven for.

Within this generous orbit,
This seemingly endless cavalcade
Of time and opportunity,
The truth is Today is like any other,
Tis ours to hold.

And as the dawning sun
Rises once again
To etch yet another notch
On this, our tentative transit
Beneath the heavens,
Why not
Make it the moment
To finally claim our shape,
To follow the very scent of our being
And live the rest of our days
More fluidly like this forever,
With a heart that's hungry to give,
With blood that remains hot and thin,
In full flow...

Surely, far better this
Than the sorry lesson
Of the torpid constituencies
All around us?
Content to insist instead
On cautious retention
Of the safe and the material,
Hollowed out, as they are,
By petty ambition
For the paper thin reassurance
Of all that is static
And therefore transient.

A jaundice of short term, selfish greed
Versus the telling ache of the soul

See what we stand to lose,
Given this veneer of comfort.
And, in its wake,
The tarnish of self deceit and compromise
That only stains our heart.

It should never be so.

But at least
I am here with you now
To share this point of acceptance,
As well as the precious tears
Of joy and release
You are weeping.

And so our odyssey begins...

The day is done
And no one is immune,
It's true.

That sense of a voyage
Slips seamlessly past,
For there is a finite beginning
And end to everything.

And yet a sense of connection,
A bejewelled purpose too,
Like the child
Whose way ahead
You've already lit,
Or the lover you've yet to meet.

Many such moments
Come and go, as they must,
Melting away
Into the space we are given.

But what endures for me
Is a persistent resonance,
Some heady wish
For access again
To a sense of wonder,
In the stream of things,
That, this time round,
It might just be possible
To keep in my heart
A little longer.

So tarry with me awhile
And we will see
What we can do
To tenderly explore
Beneath the frail shell
Of all we've since become.

Trusting that, maybe within
Such smoothly sculpted casing,
And still delicately enclosed,
Might just lie the silky lustre
Of some lavish
And joyful communion,
Waiting for its chance
To grip and catch the light again.

Every new dawn is a flitter,
A speckled canvas
Of light and possibility,
Upon which
Even the saddest amongst us
Re-materialise daily as nothing,
If not indefatigable creatures of hope.

For even to be downcast
Is in itself an admission
Of such,
A telling acknowledgement
That something's slipped away
You still hanker after.

See how, all around,
The sweet breath of joy and inspiration
Patiently awaits
The lift of will it needs from you
To lease back fresh hope
To your heart,
In a world
Where such states of grace,
Whenever they are coalesce,
Have no name, no shape,
No certainty...

So be as gallant as you can,
And take the best
Of whatever might fall your way.

As if the luckiest of adventurers,
The boldest of us
Will sometimes rise up to be,
Reaching out
Towards the improbable.

For life, wherever it leads,
Will always be the same;
It begs for the best of you.

Such chances
Come round more often
Than you might imagine,
Though, when missed,
Are gone for good...

Any opportunity lost
Always leaving behind a void
That will be there for ever,
A comet's tail of disappointment
Disappearing into the darkness.
And there is nothing at all
We can do about that.

So please bear this in mind,
Won't you?
During a glorious summer,
One of the best of our lives.
Swept along, as we are now,
Like dizzy lovers
Drunk on the yeasty liquor of life.

But right now I can only see
The sadness in your eyes
And so must apologise...

Though our kinship
Still remains delicious,
Does it not?
Forever like an overdue itch,
Ripe and ready
To be scratched with abandon.

And, in so doing,
Surely we can cut deep
Into the sadness in our souls?
Releasing a riot of passion
That, when it finally
Bursts through,
Will come soft upon us,
In warm healing waves,
And, trust me,
Nothing will then
Ever be quite the same again.

It's strange,
You'd think it needn't be so,
But the ambitious swirl of romance
Can be so seductively uncertain.

And, as we follow its call -
Sunlit aspirations,
See how we chase down
Through soft,
Billowy clouds of hope,
Dreamy and voluptuously white.
And seemingly everywhere,
As if just waiting,
Benevolently,
To break our fall.

Such heady freedom!

Though, when it comes to it,
Are we not
The most foolhardy
And fragile of prey?
Rather more prone instead
To be netted or impaled
For the siren risks we take.

But should things,
Ever tumble our way,
Then, of course,
There we will be,
Unfettered and triumphant,
As if bejewelled kingfishers
Ourselves.

Suddenly levelling out,
Sweeping imperiously
Down some rushing river
Of glorious release,
And trailing
A long and glittering retinue
Of regal reflections behind us,
For just as long
As our luck might hold.

Failures of self
Tend to come back to haunt you,
If you let them.

Where once there was surety,
Now doubt lurks,
Forever knocking slyly at your door.

And, tempted as I am,
To paint my own softer,
Kinder picture of this,
Just like any other self-deceiver
That my need for static comfort
Might ever encourage me to be,
The truth is
It makes no difference.

So think of this,
Knowing that,
Whilst I too might sometimes crave
The permanent refuge
Of imagining that the past
Can, in part,
Be somehow washed away,
It can never be so...

Though endeavour still
To be as true
And steadfast as you can be,
Conscious that
What's needed is a steady gaze
Back into the void that says
You are fundamentally unshaken.

Far better this, going forward,
Than letting loss,
Suffused with dismay and regret,
Continue to leak its sorry half life away.

Sometimes the morning sun
At the window
Is all I need to carry on.

And yet, at other times,
It is as if I could believe myself
Yearning for death,
Such is the heavy stillness
That comes upon me,
Allied to that gnawing sense
Of how far short again
I've fallen
From where I'll always long to be.

In life, it often seems
As if you have no option
But to first wipe your soul
With the very opposite experience,
To have any hope
Of ever finding your way back
To whatever it is,
Just by drawing breath,
You cannot help but still hunger for.

And so,
As my life begins to empty out,
I have come to learn
It is no more and no less than this:

The alchemy of an aching soul,
Kindly fused
With a delicate but timeless sadness,
That, with such deftness,
Duly gives birth
To the certainty of pure light.

I knew just such a woman once,
She gave me everything.
Her love like a soft scream singing,
She knew how to shine.

In your heart,
And on this journey of yours,
I suspect there is a frequency
That can guide you,
If you have both the will
And humility to trust it.

Better this
Than the crumple back to despair.

For, in truth,
Are we not all the same?
Just as nature intended
Anything but venal,
As I too
Look to find my way back
To a state of grace.

And just look how
The world still sings so,
In ageless edifice
Of careful devotions.
The selfless valour and discernment
Of times past, encrypted within,
And acting as precious clues,
Designed, as they once were,
To speak to the very ear of God.

As if all the while,
And centuries on,
Still looking to reassure us
That, beyond
The very vicissitudes of being alive,
Comes to us all
An infinite choice of gilded platforms
To stand upon,
Precious, personal opportunities
To reaffirm
The eternal legacy of such benevolence.

And therein is destined
To steadily accumulate
The best of your being,
In an endless, nameless sequence
Of individual generosity,
Seemingly disparate fragments
That, despite any loss of faith
Or intrusion of selfish desire,
Will still prevail
And come, in time,
To fit glitteringly together.

Linking us, and the very best
Of all our hopes for one another,
To lives long gone by.

For seeded into
This spectacular chance of ours,
Should you not
Be too afeard to embrace it,
There are still such possibilities,
So much joy
And enlightenment
Reverberating in the air.

I can't claim
To know exactly why,
And to what grand design,
If any,
But, just as surely as the stars
Glow in the night sky,
This is how it is.

And however burdened
Or otherwise,
However fortunate or otherwise
We perceive ourselves to be;
Indeed whatever our story,
Our defining moments
Of pain and delight,
There will always be so many
Wonderfully intricate acts
Of knowing thoughtfulness
Left behind to nurture us.

And, in all this,
I can't help but feel
The collective sigh,
The smiles of ancient souls
That bless this,
Our space to live and learn
And urge us on
To shine again...

I can still remember how it was.

Where once suffocating darkness
Held me down,
Pinned to the thinnest of expectation,
Suddenly there was broad, fresh hope
In coursing rivulets of light and beauty
Beyond compare.

Curious, isn't it though?
How those of us, still yearning
And once so close
To glorious discovery,
Can often end up
Being so far away again...

And just what to do now,
To bridge the chasm
Between one sweet point of release
And the next?

But this is assuredly
As it has to be though,
Nature's genius bursting.

After all
Blossoms come and go.
And ours was such a delicious risk.
My being abruptly and altogether
Ecstatic and be-stilled.

A state of grace,
However short-lived,
That can never be expunged.

An incontrovertible truth.

And where once there was a void,
Now at least there are
Seeds of splendour,
Becalmed belief for another time.

When previously there was always
A tendency to rein in,
To hold back,
One seemingly endless summer
Our joy stretched close to breaking point.

The world was briefly askew
With all that came upon us then
So sweetly,
The sun forever dawning bright
And warm,
All the while knowing
The long winter months still lay ahead.

Nothing we are given in this world
Is ever as immutable as this, though.

For there can be no law of nature,
No science,
No aberrant infliction of human will
That unchained
The soul cannot conquer,
Simply sweep away, should it chose to.

And whenever the luminescence
From that glorious blaze
Starts to glow,
To seep out, even a little,
Into the ether,
Then for me, there it is again!
The temptation
To burst open altogether.

Already
I ache for all the lives
I will never be a part of.

The youngest
Of all whom we love
Are so sweet an addiction.
For through them
Everything is sparkling and new,
We see life afresh once more.

I wonder if, so inspired,
You too are ready now
To wave your own wand
Of exuberance around again,
Whilst you still can...
For surely, in this purpose,
Young or old,
We are all intractably entwined together?

Sometimes though
That sense of liberation
Feels like it's been too long coming
And speaks of subliminal sadness,
A catalogue of losses
From a long time living,
That already require plunging deep
To recover from.

And so draws nearer
The twilight of our heart.

But Oh!
If we were just left to be,
Cocooned
On the balmy, becalmed surface,
As innocent infants again,
Forever seeking
To find our true shape.

To ascend,
To live, moment to moment,
In such an easy way
That truly captures the day.

To be fully assimilated,
Would that we could,
Before our time is gone
And behind us forever...

My sense, in all this,
Is that I am, just like you,
Destined to play my part.
And leave,
In the nature of my departure at least,
Some kind of sweet message behind
In the fathomless pattern I make.

A filigree of a life.

Clearly
The possibility of damage
Is ever present.

And on the horizon,
Dark stains of such
On the fabric of time
Are obvious enough.

But, for all that,
To dream of doing more,
While you still can,
Just has to be...

By all means,
We are free to spend an age,
Should we wish,
An entire lifetime even,
Wallowing in precisely
Where we are.

But however daunting
Change may look,
As we cast our gaze ahead,
We must still step up.

So take heart,
Knowing that this we owe
Uniquely to ourselves,
And all the blessings
That await us still.

For belief is the closest
To salvation we have.
And fear
Forever spits in the eye of fools,
Knowing that,
To whatever gloomy, languorous nadir
We might sometime succumb,
Unchained,
Our souls can still
Glow, like fire flies in the night,
Bringing paradise
That much closer to view.

Take pity,
As you should,
For those who are lost.
And look to find space
In your soul
To conjure a warm smile,
Just for them.

Knowing that,
Even those
We might otherwise rush
To consider evil,
Or subsumed by darkness,
Are made so
By the very chamber they inhabit.
A vessel that includes us too!

And that insight
Brings things much closer
To view, I think.
Suggesting that
The ultimate mortal sin
Is perhaps not
What we sometime
Might imagine it to be.

But instead simply having
A stiff, impervious heart,
A lack of compassion...

Something none of us,
For just as long as
We breathe
And still gladly accept
The sunlight of another day,
Can ever escape responsibility for.

Far, far away
From the prescient detritus of life
And that damned constant,
Haranguing choir,
Swelled only by the resentful,
Seeking as they do
To plague the quest of any aspirant.
Funny how it comes upon you,
So suddenly, and in clumps,
Just like its close bosom buddy
Misfortune,
The happenstance of despair.

Oh, to be magically and abruptly
That content with yourself
And all that surrounds you.
Such a sweet chance,
God given,
To be disproportionately happy.

And so, all at once,
There it is,
Nestled tearfully
In your very own hands,
Just looking at you.
The alchemy of metamorphosis:
Of something, once base
And blood ridden,
Now turned to gold.
Suffused with love,
Soft malleted...

A brand new bloom
Burst open, grown
From all you've dared to learn
And yearn for,
The sacred bequest
Of times long spent with your heart
That saturate and illuminate you now
So completely.

Look where we find ourselves...

No surprise then,
Given all we stumble across,
That we live our lives
Uncertain and tentative,
All the while wondering whether
This extended experience of ours
Is some kind of soporific dream
Sent to becalm us,
Given the sudden shock
Of our impromptu existence.

Or maybe better still?
A series of frenzied delusions,
Stoked up by the sheer excitement
Of somehow mysteriously
Continuing to be here,
In time and space,
And apparently alive!

Though whatever
The penetrating truth
Of our situation,
Could we but discern it,
The trick is surely
To keep the faith
And maintain passion,
Till ones soul sparks,
Like the stars in the night sky,
That, for us all,
Are both long gone
And yet with us still.

Some times,
Overwhelmed as I am,
I am humbled
By the very thought
Of what just might be...

It is all joining up now,
Gradually gathering in
Its own coherent story.

And, as things play out,
It's hard not to be tempted
To imagine that your life
Is one long exercise
In intertwining truths,
Progressively
And teasingly uncovered.

Long twisted ribbons of light
That continue to unravel
In extraordinary patterns
That run not only
Right through
The core of times past
And your own span of existence,
But all the ages still to come

So just what is at play here,
If not some juggernaut
Of collective memory?
Or is this something
Far more complex?
More telling still, I wonder...

See how fate decrees,
That such sweet
And illuminating experiences,
Can sometime come to you,
And altogether
In charmed combination,
Becoming powerfully reminiscent
Of something,
Instinctively it feels like
You already knew,
A long, long time ago.
And that somehow,
Has, all at once,
Been magically
Re-birthed within you
Once more.

And just what
An extraordinary feeling
That is...
Such shimmering seeds
Of joy and certainty,
Miraculously made anew,
Both to raise you up
And power you on.

So that,
On the very best of days,
It can seem like
The world around you
Is now filled
With such a warm,
And welcoming frequency
So inviting,
You instantly know
Your heart
Will make it impossible
For you not to go with it...
To answer that siren call.
To step up
And fill that space
With who you truly are.

If so blessed,
This life of ours can therefore,
From time to time,
Overwhelm, as it must.
And, as a consequence,
One must learn how
To pause,
How to be truly rich.

Believe me,
There are moments when
My heart aches so
And the stunningly sculpted shape
Of a lone red kite
Flies overhead in a clear blue sky

Increasingly, it seems, these days,
Things are falling into place.

Given all we are
And are not,
Compounded by everything
We might ever dare
To dream of being,
It seems there must always be
Some struggle to remain,
To be becalmed,
To fully embrace the moment,
The lusts of life forever seeking
To barge their way in.

And always with that
Foreboding sense of pattern
That repeats itself,
Over and over again,
And goes to the very core
Of our mortal limitations,
Remembering, as we must,
Love is never lost or found,
Merely warmed within...

So yes indeed,
I thought of you this morning
And was moved...
Cried a little
For all we once had
And also for the time when our hearts
Could perhaps sing again as one,
Knowing that, year on year,
Innumerable harvests
Yield treasure still

Here we are then,
Like it or not,
Inescapably part of it all,
Every last element...

And with little option therefore
But to accept suffering
Sometimes has to be our choice,
When this world we cling to
Is so often full of sound and fury
Worth nothing at all.

Beyond this though,
Through all
The dense jungles of doubt,
And sometime despair,
There has to be the will
To shift inside,
A way forward to faith
Of some kind.

As if, this minute,
We should take everything we are,
All our talismans
And the cleared earth too,
The very ground that we stand upon,
And fashion from it
Something shiny and anew,
Of infinitely more value,
Or so we might perceive...

But in the midst of such struggles,
I am often touched
And weep little smiles of recognition,
Just remembering your face
On that first blessed day,
Recalling the significance
Of love given
And that sense of glorious pattern
Repeating itself, again and again,
Till all our energies are spent
And our lives no more.

Lost puppies?
We are no longer,
That's for sure...
Since all that's been and gone
And the very essence of you,
Left behind in so many hearts,
Is never forgotten.

And, on a day such as this,
When your world is calm,
Full of warm smiles,
And your soul is at last
Let off its string,
One cannot help but sense,
For certain,
That all the love inside you
Comes from the best of those
You've known and loved
And those who came
And went before you too...

Sweet darlings! Sweet youth!
All our hope and dreams
Derive from just that.

So, show me the wonder
Of all you've seen so far,
Stretch the day to its limit,
And let us have no guilt
Left to waste for dreaming still.

Here are some more splinters of light... A selection of extracts taken from all of Scott Hastie's distinctive poetry to date – including chosen verses from ***Selected Poetry, New Poetry, Meditations*** and ***Angel Voices.***
For full publication listing and availability go to either:
www.scotthastie.com or www.**amazon.com**

"The sea, the sea...
Man alone,
Passive, unaware
In his elemental sadness."

"How stubborn life is,
It clings like silver in our souls."

"Here, illuminated at last,
Nestles the ruddy glint of spiritual certainty;
Sweet moments of passion and healing,
Of sensual release."

"And so we smile on,
Feeding the truths we share
With a union of our souls,
Cathedral slaves of our passion
Which builds beauty amongst chaos."

"Be content to love, to dazzle in the light,
If only for moments...
And then be gone,
With gladness in your heart,
Before the creeping shadows
Claim too much your sadness at leaving."

"Every new day
Our childrens' joy is as fresh as roses,
Even the birds chatter at dawn."

"I am sad, like the hot dust on the streets
And the music of fresh fallen leaves
Caught in a sliding summer breeze."

"The searing light of morning
Asks unwelcome questions,
Fragile hopes soon blistered by daylight."

"A permanent path
That, once illuminated,
Goes ever onward – a way home..."

"Ultimately not one amongst us
Will ever be denied that,
The glimmer of a chance to shine."

"Everyday can be extraordinary
And ripe,
Like a flower burst,
If the will is there."

"On the canvas of life,
Every sweep of the brush matters,
Counts for something..."

"The light needs only our trust
And, of course, the darkness
To work its eternal alchemy."

"Sense how
Even the smooth stones ache
With stories of their own
In the shuddering light of day."

"When in love or inspired,
An eternal kiss from the divine
Awaits us all."

"Nothing that truly matters
Can ever evaporate,
Be excised,
Burnt out of your soul."

"Once spun,
The silken thread of all our aspirations
Remains intact,
It can never be broken."

"We too can repair our cracks with gold
And glow again.
Crazed by life,
More beautiful than ever before."

"For every moment of suffering,
Others will arrive
That will instead pierce you with joy."

"Open the doors of your heart and they will come...
And for every cruel arrow,
Sweet caresses of delirium also
To nourish your soul."

"The gilded spiral
Of longings within.
Our very own cathedral
That points persistently to heaven."

"To have been where you have been
And to still have joy,
Dazzling in your heart,
Now there's a thing to make the whole world smile."

"Mislaid flame of tender emotions
Rekindled.
Together we live to the point of tears,
I wouldn't want it any other way."

"A stream of primal voices
Whispering in the breeze of your heart
To urge you on."

"Be as audacious
As you wish.
By all means look to the heavens."

"In this life at least,
Our fate is rarely epic.
Maybe just as well,
Impervious heroes we are not..."

"Be brave enough to never yearn
For that you cannot hold close
In your heart forever."

"Tread lightly, cherish compassion
And live in the moment without fear."

"You, like me,
Feel the celestial gravity in your soul,
Feel the stars ache kindly,
As they wait patiently for us."

"A hallowed frequency within
That, even in your darkest hour,
You can always turn to."

"Soothing the exhaustion
In my soul,
So I can fall back skyward,
Safe in your arms,
And survive to dream again."

"Paradise is no whim.
It takes time and trust,
You see."

"Sacred space in which
To distil, like amber,
The best of your love."

"Together we all live every moment
On the very brink;
The razor's edge
Of ecstasy or disaster."

"Disparate energies come together
That have never been aligned before.
And so bound,
Is the world illuminated,
Changed forever in an instant..."

"Sublime moments refracted,
Even if only for seconds,
Caught forever in your soul."

"Birth our night into day
And bathe it clean,
So that beloved things can glow
Together in a litter of light."

"Such is true joy's absolute certainty,
Its slow lit fuse that burns holes
In the shabby shroud of death forever."

"Life, wherever it leads,
Will always be the same,
It begs for the best of you."

"I knew such a woman once,
She gave me everything.
Her love like a soft riot singing,
She knew how to shine."

"The smiles of ancient souls
That bless this,
Our space to live and learn
And urge us on to shine again..."

"Ours was such a delicious risk.
My being abruptly and altogether
Ecstatic and be-stilled."

"Where once there was a void,
Now at least there are
Seeds of splendour,
Becalmed belief for another time."

"There can be no law of nature, no science,
No aberrant infliction of human will
That unchained the soul cannot conquer,
Simply sweep away, should it chose to."

"Already I ache for all the lives
I will never be a part of."

"I am just like you,
Destined to play my part.
And leave,
In the nature of my departure at least,
Some kind of sweet message behind
In the fathomless pattern I make.

"The sacred bequest
Of times long spent with your heart
That saturate and illuminate you now
So piercingly..."

"Let us have no guilt
Left to waste
For dreaming still."